FLOUR FANTASIES

CREATIONS IN SALTED DOUGH

Christine Steinmann

δελος

CAPE TOWN

I would like to thank:

Trudé Botma of Delos who encouraged me to write this book.
My parents, without whose support I would not have been able to do this.
Our Heavenly Father, who gives us our talents and our strength.

© 1991 Delos
40 Heerengracht, Cape Town

Also available in Afrikaans as *Deegkuns*

Typography by Corrine Lancaster
Photography by André Stander
Illustrations by Christine Steinmann
Cover design by Etienne van Duyker
Translated by Ethné Clarke
Typeset in 10,5 on 11 pt Souvenir Light by Unifoto, Cape Town
Printed and bound by Associated Printing, Cape Town

First edition, first impression 1991

ISBN 1-86826-182-4

Contents

Foreword

Like me, many people will remember making salted dough articles in their childhood. Salted dough is ideal for children to play with — washable, educational, even edible. But I hope that everyone who uses this book will also discover modelling with salted dough as an art-form in its own right and as a creative hobby.

In countries such as Greece, Poland, Czechoslovakia, Russia, Spain and Germany, modelling with salted dough is an old folk art-form which can perhaps be traced back to the pre-Christian era when shaped bread and dough sculptures were sacrificed to the gods to ensure fertility. These primitive customs have long been forgotten but the tradition has been retained in Europe through the ages as a folk art. Today, modelling with salted dough is again becoming a popular hobby in Europe, especially in Germany.

I find salted dough ideal because it is so cheap and all the necessary materials are found in any kitchen and garage. What's more, it is fun to work with. Once you hold some salted dough in your hands, you cannot resist shaping it — even if only to make a round ball. One need not begin with the most difficult items but should rather choose something simple. This is more satisfying and with practice one learns to create one's own unique works of art.

I wish everybody about to try their hand at salted dough art many pleasant hours.

Christine Steinmann

Introduction

Recipe for salted dough

125 ml water
2,5 ml dry wallpaper glue
250 ml cake flour
175 ml fine salt

Note: The wallpaper glue makes the dough more elastic, but it is not essential. Leave it out if you are going to allow small children to play with the dough.

METHOD

Measure the correct quantity of water and add the wallpaper glue. Soak for about 10 minutes until the bits of glue become clear and gelatinous. Meanwhile, mix the flour and the salt. Combine all the ingredients and knead the dough thoroughly until it has a smooth texture.

The exact quantity of water depends on the type of flour and salt but the texture of the dough can easily be adjusted by kneading in a little flour or water. The surface of the dough is perfect when it feels smooth and when your fingers do not leave marks when lightly shaping a piece of dough.

For a finer dough, if the salt is too coarse: First combine the salt with the water and the glue and mix in a food processor for a few minutes.

ADDITIONAL MATERIALS

Thin copper wire, whole cloves, brown lentils, peppercorns and other seeds for decoration.

Preserving the dough

Salted dough dries out relatively quickly, especially on warm days. It is advisable to wrap the dough in a plastic bag immediately it is ready. Take out just enough to work with.

Wrapped in a plastic bag, salted dough can easily be stored in the refrigerator for a month or even longer. If kept there for too long, it develops a strange, sharp smell but can still be used. The dough is inclined to become damp when stored. Simply knead in a little additional flour.

Coloured dough

A little extra effort is required if you wish to dye the dough in advance rather than to paint it afterwards, but a completely different effect is achieved and the end result is much better. To ensure an even colour, it is usually best to mix the dye with the water before adding the glue.

Cocoa and coffee yield shades of brown that go well with the natural colour of the dough. For a dark chocolate brown (such as the tree with blossoms in Photo 6), I used about 50 ml cocoa. Because such a large quantity was re-

quired, I sieved and thoroughly combined it with the flour and salt instead of mixing it with water. The quantity of coffee powder required for a good coffee-brown shade depends on the type used. If you find that you need only a small piece of coloured dough, knead the dry coffee or cocoa powder into the prepared dough in the same way you would knead in some flour.

For other colours, I found that the cold-water fabric dye sold in small tins and used for batik yields the best results and the largest variety of colours. To dye dough, the powder must be dissolved in water. Use only a little powder – just a pinch – as the dye is very strong. If the dough has already been prepared, dissolve the powder in a few drops of water before kneading it into the dough. Knead in a little more flour at the same time to retain the correct texture.

Equipment

Like the dough, most of the necessary equipment can be found in the kitchen.

To prepare the dough: Measuring jugs and spoons, mixing bowl and spoon, food processor (optional).

To make the articles: Rolling pin, spatula (for lifting the dough), baking sheet, kitchen knife with sharp point, thin knitting needle, wooden toothpicks, coarse sieve, garlic press, wire pliers (to bend wire loops), a smooth working surface or a large tray.

General hints

- Bear in mind how you intend hanging the article and make provision for this! Put the wire loop in place before you begin the fine decorating.
- To roll dough to a specific thickness: Place the piece of dough to be rolled between two thin wooden boards (dowel rods/stacks of paper) of the correct thickness. The boards should lie close enough to the dough for the rolling pin to touch them on either side when the required thickness is achieved.
- Always shape your article directly on the baking sheet, thus avoiding having to lift the completed article onto the baking sheet later, with possible resultant damage.
- If your article has dried slightly and the parts you want to join won't adhere properly, dampen the joints with a drop of water to moisten the dough again.
- To keep a large article, such as a wreath, damp, lightly press a clean, moist sponge over the parts still to be decorated.

Baking salted dough articles

Completed salted dough sculptures should be baked in a conventional oven and it is important to do this correctly, preferably immediately, or the salt on the surface may crystallize, leaving it rough.

Grease the baking sheet with a little cooking oil or line it with a cooking bag. The latter works very well as it enables you to move an article around to make room for other items.

Allow the articles to dry out slowly in an oven set at 100 °C. This drying process takes about two to three hours for smaller articles, but large wreaths should remain in the oven overnight. Shorten the baking time by placing the article directly on the wire rack in the oven after about an hour, once it has become reasonably solid, so that the bottom is also exposed to the hot air. The article is dry right through when it is completely hard. Removing an article from the oven to test it will do no harm, but be careful not to allow an item that has hardened on the outside but that is still wet inside to cool down too much, as air bubbles may form in the dough. If air bubbles do occur, prick them from behind with a pin and rub them out after about a quarter of an hour of the baking time has elapsed and the surface of the dough is already firm.

Painting and varnishing

Once baked through, salted dough sculptures can be painted with a suitable acrylic-based paint. The paint should be diluted slightly but should not be too runny.

Varnish is essential to protect salted dough articles from the moisture in the air. Whether you use a varnish with a glossy or a matt finish depends on personal preference. Make sure you cover the whole surface, including the back, with a layer of varnish. In a damp climate a second coat can be applied but wait until the first is completely dry. Always rinse your brushes twice in turpentine to dissolve all the varnish, and then wash them with soap and water.

Preserving salted dough articles

Because salt is inclined to absorb moisture from the air, baked salted dough sculptures easily become mouldy. In a moist atmosphere they may become soft and even fall off the wall. For this reason articles should be properly varnished and kept and displayed in a dry place if at all possible. Felt can be pasted to the back for further protection.

If articles do become soft, simply bake them at 100 °C again to dry them out.

Hanging the articles

There are several possibilities.
- With small round articles, a narrow ribbon threaded through a double or single hole at the top gives a neat finish. Another possibility is to hang an article in a ribbon pasted around the outside to form a loop at the top (see Sketch 1). Paste a bow over the place where the loop is sewn together.
- Wreaths and baskets also look attractive when hung with a loop of broad ribbon. To ensure that this hangs neatly,

do not place the ribbon directly over the nail but thread it through a curtain ring which is then hooked over the nail (see Sketch 2).

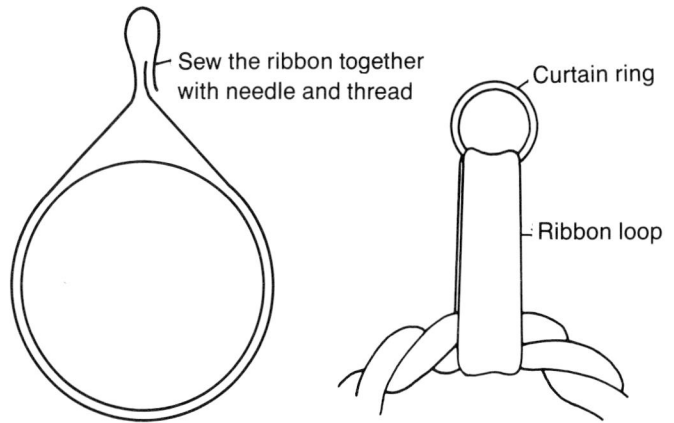

Sketch 1: Round article suspended by a ribbon loop

Sketch 2: Wreath suspended by a ribbon loop

- A wire loop pressed into the soft dough works well with any type of article. Form a loop in the middle of a piece of copper wire — about 4 cm long for smaller articles; longer for larger articles. Bend the ends to anchor the loop and to prevent it working loose (see Sketches 3 and 4). Insert into the dough and press down firmly. **Note:** With figures, wire loops should not be anchored in the head only, since the neck will not be able to support the weight of the body (see Sketch 5).
- A loop made from a strip of fabric can be attached to the completed, varnished article with contact glue (see Sketch 6).

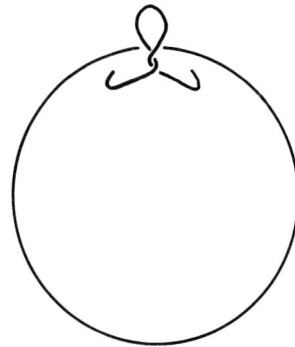

Sketch 3: Wire loop for a small article

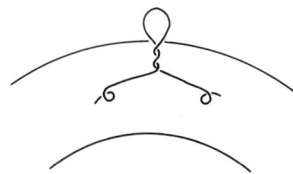

Sketch 4: Wire loop for a heavy wreath

Sketch 5: Wire loop for a free-standing figure

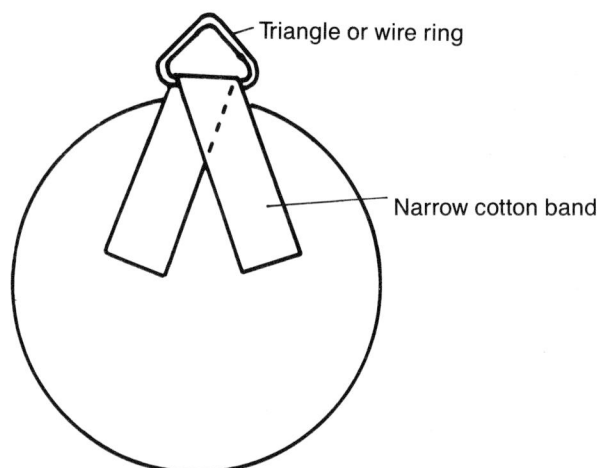

Sketch 6: Article suspended by a band glued to the back

Children-in-the-round

Because these figures of children on round backgrounds are so simple to make, they are ideal for beginners. They also make pretty gifts.

Size: 6,5 cm in diameter

Special equipment: A cooldrink glass with a thin rim and a diameter of about 6,5 cm

How to construct the figures

- Roll out the dough to a thickness of about 4 mm and use the glass to press out the round background. Trim the edges with your fingertips. Do not make more than one background at a time, as the others will dry out while you are still busy with the first one.
- Decide how you are going to hang them and either attach a wire loop or make two holes for a ribbon.
- Place a ball of dough at the top in the centre of the background for the head and flatten slightly to form a dome. Leave the eyes and mouth for later, once the hair has been attached.
- For a girl: Shape the upper part of the body. It must not be too large — at the most two-thirds of the volume of the head. Place the legs and shoes in position. Largish shoes create a cheecky effect. To shape the skirt, flatten a ball of dough, about 1 cm in diameter, with your fingers (a rolling pin is too clumsy), to form a thin piece about 1,5 mm thick. Cut off the excess dough on the sides and at the top to obtain a rectangle of the right size (see Sketch 7). It looks more natural if the bottom part, which

forms the hem of the skirt, is not cut. Carefully make folds in the skirt and attach lightly to the waist. The arms are slightly flattened balls tapered towards the shoulder and the hands are separate round balls.

- **Hint:** The stiffer the dough (but not so stiff as to form cracks), the easier it will be to shape folds and pleats in clothes and to produce the hair and other fine details.
- For a boy: The upper part of the body may be slightly larger. The trousers consist of a broad, tapered roll divided into two parts at the bottom to form the legs. Paste on thin pieces of dough to form the turn-ups of the trousers. Shape a jacket or coat from two rectangular pieces of dough by folding them over the body from the sides before attaching the arms (see Sketch 8).

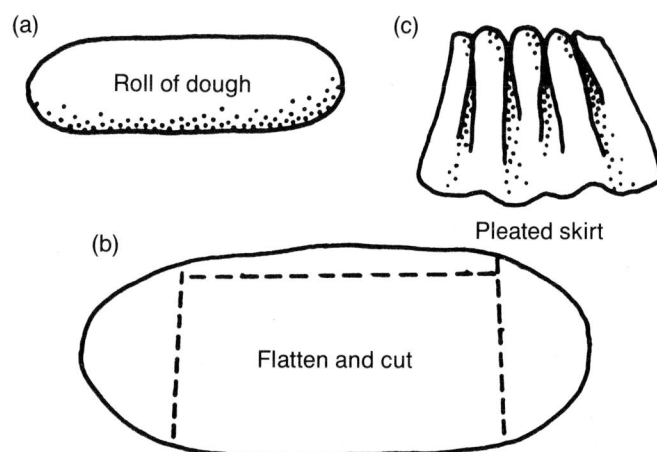

Sketch 7: How to make a skirt — e.g. figures in Photo 1, article (e)

(a)

(g)

(b)

(h)

(f)

(c)

(i)

(e)

(d)

Photo 1

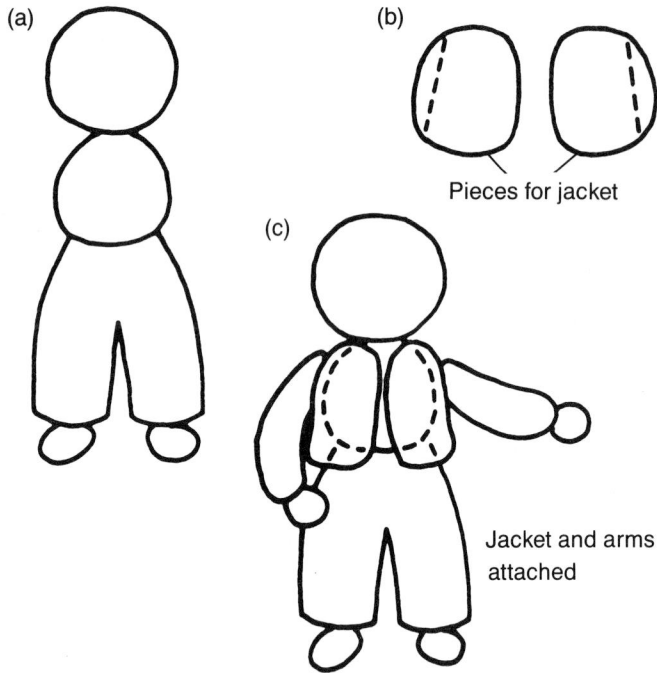

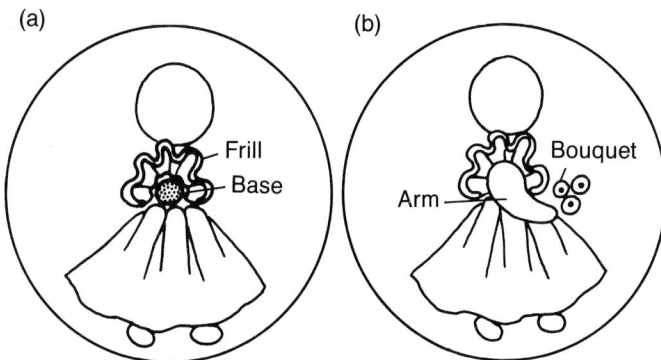

Sketch 8: How to make a jacket — e.g. figure in Photo 1, article (g)

Piece of dough for shirt in position

Dress overlaps shirt

Shoulder straps added

Cross-section of figures in Photo 1, articles (c) and (f)

Sketch 10: Girl with basket — Photo 1, article (f)

- The figures in articles (a), (c) and (f) in Photo 1 are variations on this basic method.
- The little girl in the pink dress, Photo 1, article (a), has no bodice. Make the skirt first. The frill around the arm consists of a flattened ball, 5 mm wide, which is pleated and shaped into a fan. Place a round piece of dough in the centre to serve as a base. Press the upper arm onto this base to cover it (see Sketch 9).
- The little girl with the basket in Photo 1, article (f), and the little boy with the cap in Photo 1, article (c), both in blue, are made in almost the same way. The piece of shirt under the chin simply consists of a small piece of dough tapered at the bottom. Use solid dough for the dress/trousers which are tapered slightly towards the top where they overlap with the edge of the shirt. Braces cover the place where the arms join the body (see Sketch 10).

- There are several methods for making hair:
  - Paste a thin layer of dough onto the head and use a toothpick to produce texture — see the figures in Photo 1, articles (a) and (f).
  - Press stiff dough through a coarse sieve, carefully remove the curls that form with a knife point and attach to the head — see the figures in Photo 1, articles (b) and (g).
  - Roll out very thin pieces (or press the dough through a garlic press to obtain smooth curls) and attach close together on the head — see the figures in Photo 1, articles (h) and (i).
  - Plaits consist of two twisted rolls of dough and pigtails of diamond-shaped pieces of dough textured to look like hair.

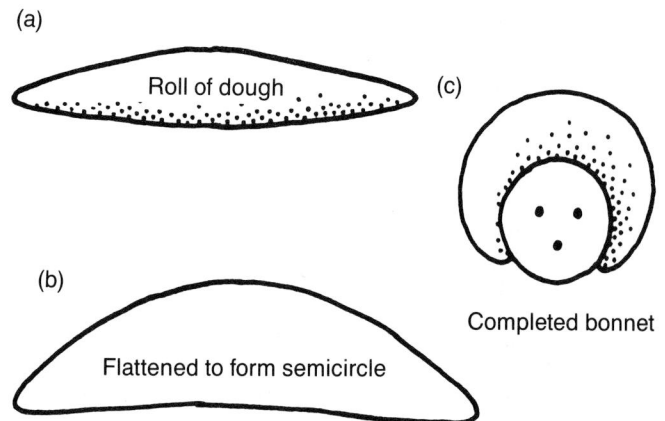

Sketch 9: How to make a figure without a bodice — Photo 1, article (a)

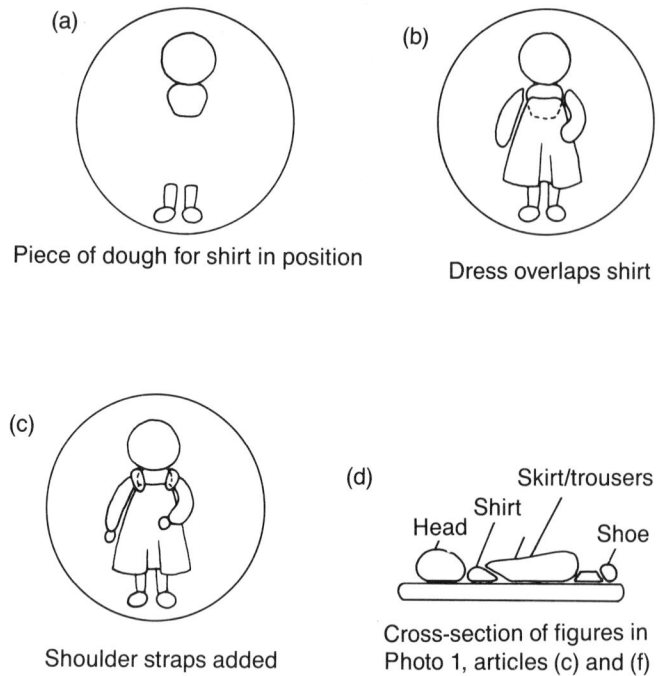

Sketch 11: How to make a bonnet

8

- Hats and bonnets consist of a thin semicircle of dough folded around the head (see Sketch 11).
- Now add accessories such as buttons, a basket, simple flowers or a cat. Do not overdo the accessories.

Painting

Because the figures are so simple, painting is important. First paint the larger areas in one or two strong, matching colours. When the paint has dried, paint the patterns on the clothes with a fine brush. A touch of white is essential, as it brings out the other colours.

A flesh colour is achieved by mixing white, a little yellow and a dash of red. Paint rosy cheeks with a runny cherry red paint while the face is still damp so that it blends into the face colour.

Articles in coloured dough

Figures and wreath in blue

This collection of figures in blue and off-white is ideal for a room with a blue colour scheme. It is also an excellent project to practise working with coloured dough.

Size: Wreath 12,5 cm in diameter; larger circle 9,5 cm in diameter; smaller circle 7,5 cm in diameter

Special equipment: Round objects with the required diameter

You will require only a small piece of dark blue dough for this project. If you intend working with coloured dough at a later stage, it is a good idea to halve the dough recipe and to dye the dough a darker shade of blue during the preparation. To obtain light blue, combine a piece of dark blue with a piece of white dough. When working with different colours, the working surface, your hands and all your equipment must be kept clean throughout to ensure that the colours remain pure.

The figures on the circles in Photo 2, articles (a), (b) and (c), are made in exactly the same way as the painted children in the previous project. If you do not have a glass sufficiently large to shape the background, use a round bowl or lightly place a cut-out cardboard disc on the rolled dough and cut around it with a knife. Because the figures are not painted, greater attention must be paid to the finer accessories shaped from different shades of coloured dough.

Bouquets such as the one held by the little boy in Photo 2, article (a), are shaped as follows: Place a piece of dough about the size of the bouquet in the place where the figure's hands would be. Shape leaves by flattening small round balls and pinching both ends to form points. Attach them in an irregular pattern around the edge of the base and press

a groove in each with the side of a knitting needle. Shape slightly smaller round balls for the flowers and press down with the point of a knitting needle to complete the bouquet (see Sketch 12).

Shape the wreath in Photo 2, article (d), from three rolls of dough, each about 40 cm long and 1,2 cm in diameter. Do not press the two ends of the plait together. Sketches 13, 14 and 15 illustrate how to join the two ends neatly.

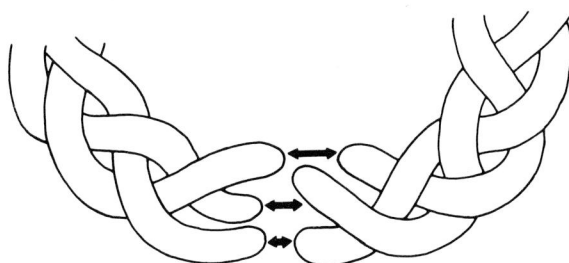

Sketch 13: How to join the plaited ends of a wreath

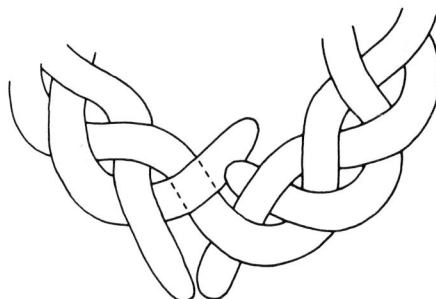

Sketch 14: Central roll of dough joined

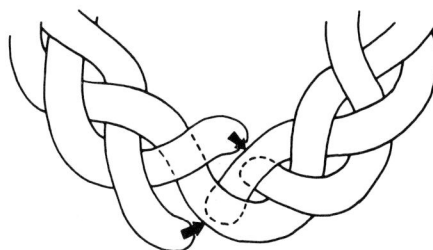

Sketch 15: Rolls on each side are cut off and folded in

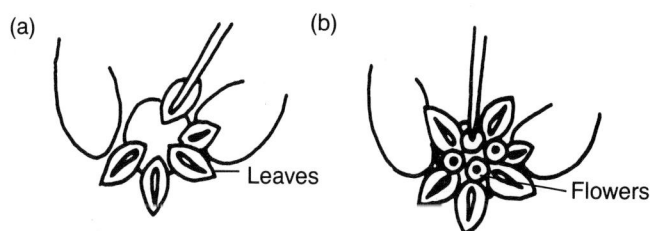

Sketch 12: How to make a bouquet

Photo 2

First join the middle rolls. To join the outer rolls, cut off the one end just where it appears under the plait and tuck the other end under the plait in the same place. Attach a wire loop for hanging. If you feel this is too complicated, cut off the two ends of the plait bluntly, press them firmly together and hang the wreath on a broad blue ribbon that covers the join.

To decorate, first shape the leaves from the white dough (see p. 11). Arrange them in five groups on the wreath. The flowers that complete the wreath each consist of a flattened ball, the edge of which has been notched with the blunt edge of a knife to form the five petals.

Figures in shades of brown

The different shades of brown in these figures were achieved by mixing the dough for articles (e), (f) and (g) in Photo 2 with coffee and for articles (h) and (i) with cocoa. Because these figures are not mounted on a background, more attention has to be paid to the way the different parts of the body are joined at the back. The neck is reinforced with a piece of dough and the body is extended to join the legs under the dress. Sketch 16 shows what the two bosom friends in Photo 2, article (e), will look like from behind. If you intend hanging any of these figures on a wire loop, the loop must be anchored into the body (see Sketch 5, p. 5).

Small pieces of dough must be used for decorating, as with the figures in blue. For the long hair of the little girls in Photo 2, articles (e) and (f), push the dough through a garlic press. The violin player's bow is a toothpick. The template for the violin is given in Sketch 17.

Sketch 16: Two figures on Photo 2, article (e), seen from behind

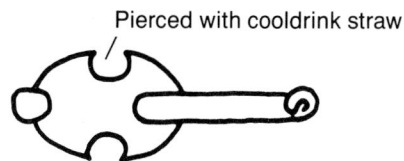

Pierced with cooldrink straw

Sketch 17: Template for violin

Flowers, leaves, fruit and baskets

Decorations such as flowers, leaves and fruit require practice and a lot of patience but the results are very satisfying.

Hints

- Use relatively solid dough. Do not try to make the leaves or petals too thin. If you want a leaf to stand erect, the dough should not be too soft or the leaf will droop.
- First shape all the main flowers or fruit of the arrangement. Shape the leaves and berries for the background as you progress.
- Now place the main fruit or flowers of the decoration lightly in position, without pressing them down. This will enable you to move them around or to tuck leaves underneath them. Arrange the leaves, flowers and berries in the spaces in between. When you have finished, press everything down firmly.

Leaves: Flatten a ball of dough, shape to form an oval and pinch the ends to form points. Place on a flat surface and etch the veins of the leaf with the blunt edge of a knife (Sketch 18).

Vine leaves: Shape three points to a leaf, with the central one slightly longer, and etch a main vein running to each point (Sketch 19).

Roses: Shape four balls of dough, with one almost double the size of the other three. Simply flatten the smaller ones. The larger one is first rolled to form an oblong, then flattened. Now roll the oblong leaf to form a cone by pressing the bottom parts together and bending open the top (Sketch 20b). Attach the other three leaves around the outside. Allow the first leaf to overlap slightly with the loose end of the rolled-up cone, the second to overlap a little over the first and so forth. To make a larger rose, increase the number of loose leaves attached to the cone. For a rosebud,

Sketch 18: Leaves   Sketch 19: Vine leaf

use only the oblong rolled-up leaf and replace the three round petals with five small, green sepals — see Sketch 20e.

Blossoms: Flatten five balls of dough so that they are slightly thinner on the one side. Arrange in a circle with their thinner sides towards the centre (Sketch 21). The stamens consist of a few 5 mm long curls made by pressing the dough through a coarse sieve.

Daisies: Shape these by arranging narrow, tapered leaves (at least seven) in a star pattern, and placing a small ball in the centre (see Sketch 22).

Sunflowers: Shape these in the same way, but make the centre larger and the petals smaller (Sketch 23).

Blue daisies: The centres of the blue daisies in Photo 3, article (b), consist of yellow dough pressed through a sieve and then lightly shaped to form a ball.

The pink flowers with four petals in Photo 3, article (b) are shaped in the same way as the forget-me-nots in Photo 2, article (d), by making notches around the edge of a round piece of dough (Sketch 24). Use the blunt edge of a knife while holding the flower between the thumb and forefinger of your other hand.

Berries: Press a small hole, or for variation, a small seed, into a round ball (Sketch 25).

Apples: Use larger balls and finish off with cloves. Cut a whole clove in half. Use the stem section to form the stem of the apple and the head of the clove to form the little flower on the apple (Sketch 26).

Pears: Roll a piece of dough between the palms of your hands to form a pear shape and finish off with cloves as for the apples (Sketch 27).

Grapes: Shape a flattish triangle of dough a little smaller than the bunch is going to be. Cover this base with small round balls and finish off with tendrils (Sketch 28).

Baskets

Sizes: Large basket 14 cm high with handle; small basket 9,5 cm high

Roll out some dough and cut out the shape of the basket, leaving an extra strip of dough at the top. Flatten this strip of dough, which should be more or less the shape of the intended arrangement, with your fingers to serve as a base on which to attach the fruit or flowers. (Template 1 on page 29 can be used for the 9,5 cm basket.)

Smooth the edges of the basket with your fingertips and use a wooden stick to produce the woven effect. Twist two rolls of dough around each other to form the base and the handle and attach to the basket. Make sure that the handle is attached firmly, since these joins have to support the weight of the basket.

Now arrange the contents of the basket. First place the main flowers or fruit in position so that the leaves can be arranged around them. Begin with the outer leaves and work towards the centre. Note that the leaves between the roses in Photo 3, article (d), do not necessarily have to lie flat.

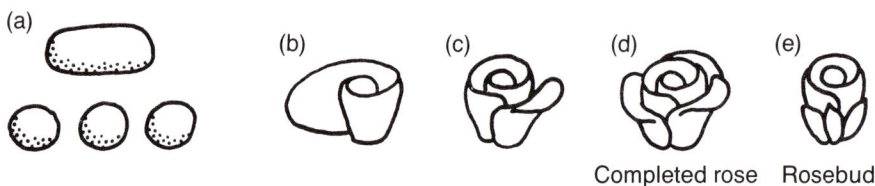

Sketch 20: How to make a rose

Sketch 21: Blossom

Sketch 22: Daisy

Sketch 23: Sunflower

Sketch 24: Forget-me-not with variations

Sketch 25: Berries

Sketch 26: Apples

Sketch 27: Pear

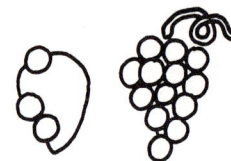

Sketch 28: Bunch of grapes

12

(a)

(b)

(c)

(d)

Photo 3

Photo 4

14

Wreaths

A wreath made of salted dough, possibly combined with dry seeds and flowers, makes a striking decoration for any room.

Plaited wreath with roses and berries

Size: 19 cm in diameter

Roll out three pieces of dough, each about 1,7 cm in diameter and 40-50 cm long, and plait them. To fold one roll over the other, lift the entire length of the roll carefully over the first one to prevent the roll from stretching or breaking. As the decoration will cover the join, the ends can be pressed together, and if the plait is not long enough, a piece of dough can be inserted between the ends. The join must be as thick and as wide as the rest of the plait.

First shape the roses (see pp. 11-12) and the two large poppy-like flowers. These consist of a flat, round piece of dough, 40 mm in diameter. Pinch the centre of this circle of dough from the back with the thumb, forefinger and middle finger of your left hand, folding it to the inside in three places. Use your right hand to shape the folds. Place these flowers in position and fill the spaces in between with berries, small flowers and leaves. Each berry is made of a ball of dough with a canna seed pressed into it. The other bunches consist of small flowers with three leaves each and a canna seed in the centre. Each bunch is mounted on top of a piece of dough so that the roses do not stand out too much above the berries.

Wreath with brown roses

Size: 17 cm in diameter

The wreath is shaped on a smooth, slightly flattened ring of dough. Remember to attach a wire loop. I found it easier to first shape the roses from stiff brown dough and then to place them lightly in position. In this way one can see exactly how to arrange the leaves and buds. Finally press the roses onto the wreath with the aid of a knitting needle inserted unobtrusively between the rose leaves where the marks cannot be seen.

Wreaths with seeds and dried flowers

Sizes: Both 12 cm in diameter

These wreaths are formed by twisting two rolls of dough around each other. Do not worry about the joins as the decoration will cover them.

Two largish, interesting seeds form the focal point of the wreath on the left in Photo 4, the other seeds radiating from them towards the sides. Try to follow the curve of the wreath in your arrangement. To make the wreath with the dried flowers, simply begin in the centre and work towards the sides. Because the flowers have to be placed close together, pliers come in handy for gripping the flower stems while inserting them into the dough.

These wreaths can be baked in the same way as other dough sculptures. Handle with care though, since the heat makes the plant material very brittle. When you varnish wreaths with dried seeds and grasses, take into consideration which seeds will look attractive with a coat of varnish and which should rather be left unvarnished.

Trees and cottages

Designs for trees and cottages present many possibilities — either realistic or purely decorative.

Farm boy under an apple tree

Size: 22 cm high

Shape the trunk and roots of the tree from soft coffee-coloured dough. Use a wooden stick to produce the texture of the bark. For the crown, roll out some white dough to a thickness of about 4 mm and cut out an irregular disc, about 12 cm in diameter. Attach it to the trunk and insert a wire loop at the top. To give a little more shape to the crown of the tree, roll out a piece of dough to a thickness of 6 mm and cut out a second, smaller circle (9 cm in diameter).

Place this on top of the larger one and make a sloping edge. Cover the crown with leaves of white dough and apples of light coffee-coloured dough, working from the outside to the inside. Place the little boy with his cocoa-coloured jacket in the curve of the trunk. Note that his legs consist of two separate rolls. Use cloves to finish off the apples and the boy's hat.

Dark brown tree

Size: 14 cm high

The dough for this tree is dyed with cocoa. The lighter and darker shades develop automatically as the dough dries.

Roll out the dough to a thickness of 4 mm. Trace Tem-

Photo 5

16

plate 2 on page 29 onto thin paper and cut it out. Place the pattern lightly on the dough and cut out the outline of the tree (ignore the leaves extending beyond the edges). Smooth the edges with your fingertips. Add a wire loop or hole for hanging. First arrange the branches, then the leaves and birds and finally the balls and berries on the tree shape. If you wish, mark their positions on the tree beforehand by placing the template on the base and pricking holes all along the lines with a pin.

Cottage and tree in pastel colours

Sizes: Cottage 15,5 cm high; tree 12,5 cm high

Special equipment: A teaspoon with a roundish point to shape the roof tiles

Roll out a piece of white dough to a thickness of about 4 mm. Trace Template 3 on page 29 and Template 6 on page 30 and cut out these shapes. Mark details — especially the eaves, door and windows of the cottage — with a pin by pricking along all the lines through the paper into the dough. Smooth the edges of the cut-out shapes and insert wire loops in the crown of the tree and at the top corners of the cottage roof.

Shape the tree as described above for the chocolate-brown tree.

The first step in decorating the cottage is to make a tile pattern with the tip of a teaspoon in the roof section. Shape the eaves from a roll of white dough, and place a thinner yellow one next to it. Cut out an arch for the door from very thinly rolled-out dough and press vertical grooves into it with a thin knitting needle. Frame the door with a yellow roll. For the windows, roll out some dough very thinly and cut out a cross. Use a thin white roll for the top and sides of the window frame and a thicker roll for the windowsill. Finish off with decorations such as flowers, bows and birds. A loose piece of fence consisting of four flattened rolls connects the tree and cottage to form an attractive picture.

Decorated tiles

Two landscapes

Size: 12 cm x 10,5 cm

Roll out some dough and cut out the tiles for these charming scenes. Attach the wire loops.

For the trunk of the tree with blossoms in the top picture in Photo 6, use soft dough which can easily be textured. Use green dough pressed through a garlic press for the grass in both pictures. Cut off the curls with a sharp knife when they reach a length of 4 mm or 5 mm. Make the sheep's wool in the same way, but shorter.

The ploughed field in the bottom landscape is a very thin piece of dough etched with parallel lines. To achieve depth, vary the texture of the grass. Make that on top of the hill very short and fine and that around the sheep's legs longer, with other plants added as well. Shape the sheep individually and add to the landscape at the end. Shape a disc of dough as large as the sheep's body and attach the legs to the back. Use the garlic press to make the wool covering the body. Keep a bit of wool and attach it between the sheep's ears after the head has been placed in position.

Tile with birds

Size: 22 cm x 6,5 cm

The three birds are a sparrow, a hoopoe and a crow and are all shaped in the same way with a body that tapers towards the tail, a round head, a triangular piece of dough for the tail feathers and a semicircle for the wing. Make the eyes, beaks and the patterns on the feathers with pieces of coloured dough. I made the circle in the eye with the back of a ballpoint cartridge. Complete the background by adding coiled twigs bearing bunches of berries.

Photo 6

Photo 7

Pictures in frames

The idea of mounting your salted dough creations in simple wooden frames will open new design possibilities. Use illustrations in children's books and birthday cards for inspiration. Because salted dough pictures are three-dimensional, you should strive for a good balance between the thickness of the dough used for your picture and the thickness of the frame. Be particularly careful when you use curtain rings as frames – do not place the picture too far back in the frame which will otherwise dominate the picture. The thicker parts of the design should be about the same thickness as the frame. Features of the picture could even extend a few millimetres beyond the frame.

Pictures framed in curtain rings

Special materials: Wooden curtain rings (about 8,5 cm in diameter), sandpaper, stiff cardboard, dark brown felt, clear adhesive, small hooks

Sand the curtain ring with sandpaper and then varnish. When the first layer has dried, it can be lightly sanded again and given a second layer of varnish for a smooth finish. Cut a circle, 7,5 cm in diameter, from the cardboard to fit neatly onto the back of the curtain ring. Cut two or three felt circles (together they should have a thickness of 4 mm). Make the largest one 6,5 cm in diameter and each of the other two about 2 mm smaller than the previous one. The felt layers help to build up the background slightly so that the picture will not be too far back in the frame.

Paste the layers of felt onto the cardboard. This will form the base on which to construct your picture (protect the felt from the dough with a plastic bag). Place the frame over the base occasionally as the work progresses to get a total image. The toadstools are semicircles shaped from two pieces of dough in different colours, with stalks added. First position a piece of white dough as a base below the stalks and attach the grass to this base. The ferns in the right-hand curtain ring picture on Photo 7 are shaped from a flattened roll of dough, tapering towards the top. Make notches along both sides, etch a vein in the middle and roll up the end.

When you have baked and varnished all the parts, glue the ring to the background and then paste the design onto the felt. Screw a small hook into the top of the curtain ring for hanging.

Sculptures in picture frames

Special materials: A picture frame, plywood, short nails, a small hook

The most suitable frame for this purpose is a slightly broad wooden frame with a bevelled edge (sloping towards the inside). To make the frame slightly deeper, replace the usual backing, which is inclined to fit into the back of the frame, with a sturdy piece of plywood (or very stiff cardboard) which must be the same size as the outer edge of the frame. Use small nails to attach this backing.

Now construct your picture inside the frame. An interesting effect is achieved if some parts of the picture extend beyond the frame (like the trees in the pictures in Photo 7). It is essential to line the wooden frame with a cooking bag, as the dough portion of the picture has to be removed from the frame after it has been baked. (The dough picture has to be baked in the frame to ensure that it still fits perfectly afterwards.)

After baking, remove the dough pieces and varnish. The background of the frame can be painted, covered with fabric, or a landscape photo from an old calendar can be pasted onto it, as in Photo 7. When you have glued the picture into the frame, screw a small hook into the top of the frame so that the picture hangs squarely.

Mobiles

Any objects suspended from a mobile should look equally attractive from all sides. This restricts one to a certain extent, but the following are two good ideas.

Heart mobiles

Special materials: The inner wooden ring of an old embroidery frame (or any suitable ring about 12 cm in diameter), broad red ribbon about 60 cm long, red thread and a needle, an empty tin, plate shears, small square-nosed pliers, Prestik, small metal ring for hanging the mobile

It is easy to make the cutters needed for pressing the triangles and diamonds into the hearts. Using the shears, cut strips about 6 mm wide out of the tin. Bend a 1,5 cm long strip to form a triangle with 6 mm, 6 mm and 3 mm sides respectively. For the diamond with its four 5 mm sides you will need a 2 cm long strip.

Patterns for five hearts of various sizes (Templates 4 and 5) appear on pages 29 and 30. Trace the patterns and use them to cut out eight heart shapes from a piece of white and a piece of red dough rolled out to a thickness of 2 mm. I used white dough for the largest heart, red dough for the smallest heart and, for variation, both colours for the three medium sizes. Place the cut-out hearts on a baking sheet before commencing the decorating. Make a border around each heart, using either small red and white balls, or a red and a white roll twisted together. Make a pattern of little holes in each heart and remember to make the hole at the top for hanging.

After baking and varnishing the hearts, tie a piece of red thread (about 50 cm long) to each one. Cover the wooden ring with the red ribbon by wrapping the ribbon neatly around it and securing the end with needle and thread. Attach three pieces of red thread, equally spaced to the top of the ring with a few sturdy stitches. Hang the ring horizontally by these threads – not too high up and above a soft cushion, to prevent mishaps while you work. For the present, attach the hearts, excluding the largest one, by their threads to the wooden ring with Prestik. Adjust the lengths of the threads until you are satisfied and then mark each thread at the right length. Take the ring down and attach each thread to the ribbon wrapped around the ring with a number of sturdy stitches. Hang the largest heart right in the centre by knotting its thread, together with the three threads for hanging, onto a small metal ring.

Guineafowl mobile

Special materials: Strong white nylon thread, thin but strong sticks cut from wood or, preferably, Spanish reed, contact glue, copper wire

Use Template 7 on page 31 and cut out five bird shapes from a piece of dough rolled out to a thickness of 4 mm. Smooth the edges and remember to attach a wire loop to each one. Make thinnish rolls and press them flat onto the body to form the wing and tail feathers. Flatten a round ball the size of a pea and attach it to the head just behind the beak. Repeat on the other side of the bird. Bend a 9 cm long roll of dough so that it almost forms a triangle, and attach the two loose ends to the body a small distance from each other, one on each side, to form the legs. Make a few beads of different sizes from salted dough. Use a needle about 1 mm thick to pierce a hole through each one, and thread them onto thin copper wire before baking. They must not touch each other.

After you have baked the guineafowl, paint them but leave the legs and beaks unpainted. Paint the body black, the comb reddish-brown (red with a tiny bit of black and/or blue) and the part around the eye powder blue (blue with a touch of white and red). When the paint has dried, paint the spots and the eyes. Paint about half the beads black.

When you have finished painting and varnishing, tie a thread of about 30 cm to each guineafowl. Also tie a thread to the centre of each stick. (The length of the sticks is given in Sketch 29.) Arrange the entire mobile on a rug or blanket as shown in Sketch 29. Thread the beads onto the nylon strands and glue each in position with contact glue at the correct height. Make a mark on the strands at the correct length and tie them to the ends of the sticks. Place a drop of glue on each knot tied to the end of a stick, but do not glue those in the centre of the sticks. When the glue is dry, carefully lift the mobile by the top thread and hang it above something soft. Adjust the knots of the threads from which the sticks are suspended until they balance and glue them in that position.

Photo 8

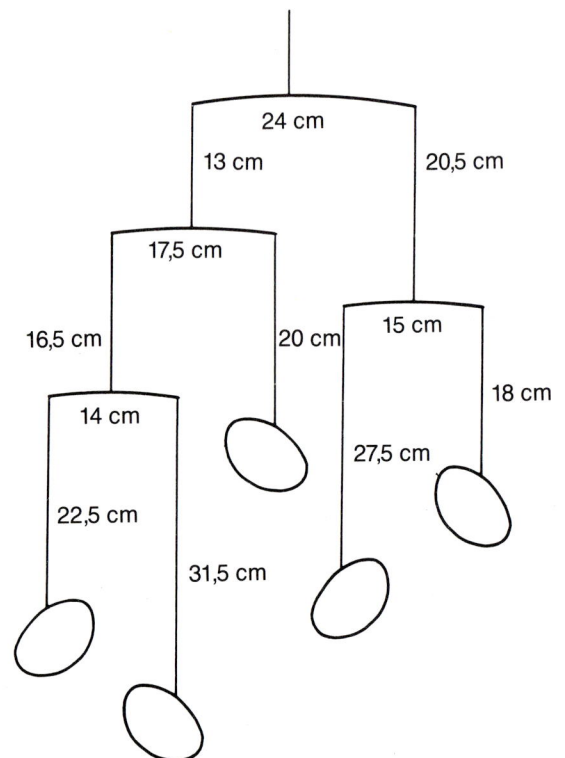

Sketch 29: Guineafowl mobile

Photo 9

Grandma and Grandpa at the window

Size: 20 cm high

Special materials: A piece of broad lace, a small acorn cap for Grandpa's pipe, two toothpicks for knitting needles, a scrap of black wool, copper wire for spectacles

Shape a roll of dough, 1,2 cm in diameter, and cut off two 13 cm pieces and one 18 cm piece. Place these rolls side by side, with the longest one in the middle and about 7,5 cm space between each. Flatten the last 5 mm on both ends of each roll but do not allow them to become wider. Shape another roll, slightly thicker and about 26 cm long, and place it in a curve from the top of one short roll to the top of the other short one. Attach it to the end of the long roll in the middle and to the ends of the shorter rolls by pressing the flattened parts firmly to the back of it (Sketch 30).

To prevent the window frame at the top and the windowsill at the bottom from bulging where they cross the vertical rolls, do the following: Cut broad wedges in the three vertical rolls of dough at the point where the window frame will cross them — about 13 cm from the bottom — without cutting through the roll (Sketch 31a). Fill up the distance be-tween the wedges by cutting two pieces from a thinnish roll (about 7 mm thick) to fit exactly into the space between the vertical rolls and place them there. Repeat for the windowsill, although the wedges are not necessary because the ends have been flattened (see Sketch 31b). Now shape the 1,5 cm thick, 21 cm long rolls for the top frame and the windowsill, place them in position and press down firmly. Make notches in the windowsill and the arch with a knitting needle and insert the crossbeams in the top part (Sketch 32).

It is easy to make the Grandma and Grandpa. Do not make them too small or too flat in relation to the window frame. Add the cat and the birds. Grandma's spectacles, knitting needles (without the knitting) and Grandpa's pipe are baked together with the dough. Make sure you will be able to remove the knitting needles and spectacles after baking to facilitate the painting and varnishing of the figures. Before putting the knitting needles back in place, knit a few stitches on fine needles and slip them over the tips of the toothpicks. Finish off the window with a lace curtain.

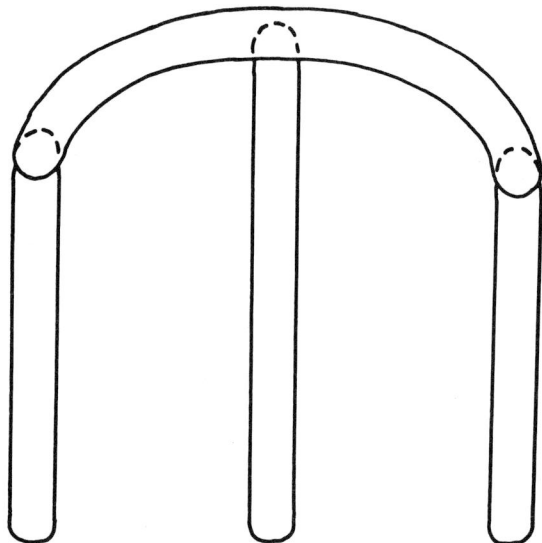

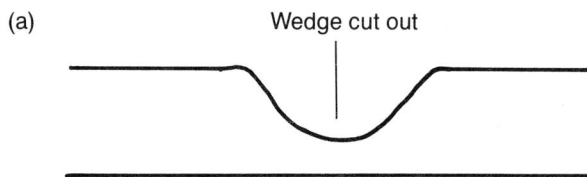

Sketch 30: Arch attached to vertical rolls of dough

(a)

Wedge cut out

(b)

Wedge cut out

Thinner rolls for filling

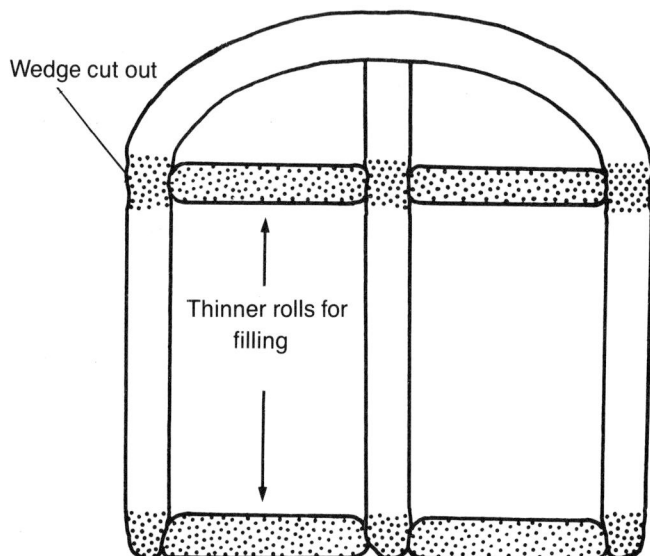

Sketch 31: Place thinner rolls of dough between vertical rolls for reinforcement

Photo 10

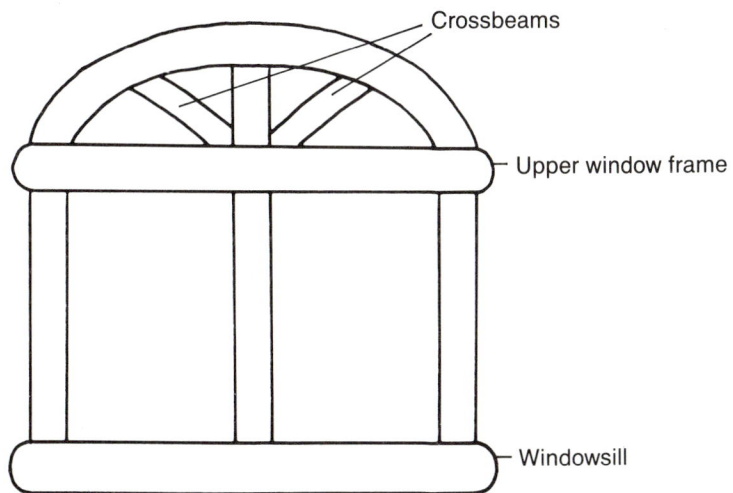

Sketch 32: Completed window frame

Candleholders and animals

Decorate your table at Christmas, Easter or birthday celebrations with candles in salted dough candleholders, or with these bunnies and hedgehogs or give them to a friend as a gift.

Hint: Before putting the candleholders in the oven, check that the candle still fits and that the decorations are not in the way.

Candleholder with simple flowers

Size: Inner diameter 4 cm; outer diameter 7 cm

Roll out a piece of dough to a thickness of 4 mm and press out a circle with a diameter of 6 cm. Make a roll of dough, about 8 mm in diameter and 15 cm long. Press it onto the edge of the circle of dough and rub the join with a wet finger until it disappears. Shape another roll, slightly longer and about half as thick, and press it around the rim of dough. The rolls of dough should touch each other. Make five marks at regular intervals on the thick roll of dough. Arrange five leaves and two simple flowers on each mark. The flowers each consist of a flattened ball of dough divided into three petals by notches in the edge and finished off with a clove in the centre.

Candleholder from coloured dough

Size: Inner diameter 5,5 cm; outer diameter 9 cm

Roll out a piece of dough to a thickness of 4 mm and cut out a circle with a diameter of 7,5 cm. Make a plait about 25 cm long from three rolls, each 1 cm thick. Join the ends of the circle as neatly as possible (see pp. 9 and 11 for instructions and sketches). Attach the plait to the edge of the circle so that the edge is completely covered.

Decorate the plait with leaves of green dough and coral-red blossoms (see pp. 11-12). Use white dough pressed through a sieve for the stamens and attach a few of the curls to the centre of the flower. The buds consist of two petals partly overlapping and three very narrow dark green sepals.

Large candleholder with fruit and leaves

Size: Inner diameter 6,5 cm; outer diameter 9,5 cm

Roll out a piece of dough to a thickness of 4 mm and cut out a circle with a diameter of 9,5 cm. Press a 12 mm thick roll of dough about 5 mm into the edge of the circle of dough. Taper the roll of dough towards the edge of the circle to obtain a smooth sloping surface for the decorations. Divide the circumference of the edge into three equal parts by making three marks. Divide each third into three parts in the same way. On each of the nine marks on the edge, alternate apples, pears or grapes (see p. 12 for how to make the fruit). Fill in the remaining background with ordinary leaves and place vine leaves around the grapes. Finally, stack balls of dough all along the highest part of the edge. Make a hole in each ball with a knitting needle. Finish off the apples and pears with cloves.

Easter bunnies

Use a stiff dough for these Easter bunnies and bake them slowly and for a long time in the oven to dry out thoroughly.

Make a ball of dough with a diameter of about 4 cm for the body. Shape the body like an egg and flatten the sides slightly. Shape the head from a ball of dough with a diameter of about 1,8 cm by flattening it slightly on the sides and tapering it towards the nose. Now make five balls of dough for the legs and tail and attach these to the body. Place the tail more or less opposite the head. For a reclining bunny, the back legs must be close to the tail and the front legs a short distance from the head. For a bunny standing on its back legs, place the back legs about halfway between the head and the tail and the front legs directly below the head. The dough for the ears must be at least 3 mm thick to ensure that they will stand erect. Wedge a piece of rolled paper between the back and the ears to support them until they are baked hard enough to stand by themselves. Black glass beads for eyes and a few licks of paint after baking complete the bunny.

Hedgehogs

Special materials: Seeds of a liquidambar tree

The seeds of a liquidambar tree are used to form the bodies of these hedgehogs. Place the stem side of the seed facing down. First remove the worst prickles where the head and legs are to be attached to the seed. Use a knitting needle and fill the holes in the seed at these places with dough in order to have a base on which to attach the head and legs. Make sure that the head, in particular, will cover the filling. To form the head, press a ball of dough onto the seed and shape the snout. Attach four oblong balls of dough at the bottom of the seed for legs. Press two black beads into the head for eyes.

Photo 11

Choir boys and Christmas decorations

Decorations for a Christmas tree

It is always fun to make your own Christmas tree decorations.

WREATHS

Size: 6 cm in diameter

Shape two rolls of dough, each about 9 mm in diameter and about 18 cm long. Twist them around each other and form a ring. Where the ends meet, press the one lightly onto the other one − this should be neat enough. Make a loop with 4 cm of copper wire and insert it into the wreath at the join.

Decorate the wreath with an arrangement of dried seeds combined with leaves of salted dough. Press a row of small seeds, such as lentils, into one of the rolls of dough. To pre-

vent the lentils from falling out of the dough, glue them in position after the wreath has been baked.

STARS, HEARTS, TREES AND CIRCLES

Special equipment: Biscuit cutters in different shapes, a thimble, a knitting needle, an empty tin, plate shears and small wire pliers with a blunt nose

Make your own cutters for pressing the triangles and diamond shapes into these articles (see p. 19 for instructions on how to make hearts for a mobile).

Roll out the salted dough about 2 mm thick on a floured surface. Press out the different shapes with biscuit cutters. Using a spatula, carefully lift each shape onto a baking sheet. Use the triangle, diamond, thimble and knitting needle to make a pattern of holes on each dough shape. See Templates 8, 9 and 11 on pp. 31 and 32 for a few ideas. To

25

make sure that the knitting needle penetrates the dough, turn the shape round and open the hole from the back. These shapes are baked and varnished in the same way as other articles and hung on the Christmas tree with cotton thread.

ANGELS

Size: 6,5 cm high

You will need 7 cm of copper wire for each angel. Fold the wire in half without bending the ends. Slightly flatten a ball of dough with a diameter of about 13 mm for the head. Roll out a piece of dough to a thickness of 3 mm to make the dress. The neck of the dress is about 1 cm wide; the dress becomes wider towards the bottom and the hem forms a curve. Insert the two ends of the wire, which has been folded in half, right through the head so that only a small loop sticks out (Sketch 33a). Bend the ends of the wire and insert them at the neck of the dress until the dress touches the head. By anchoring the wire in the dress one ensures that the neck has less weight to support (Sketch 33b).

Now add the wings and other details. Press a few folds into the dress with the side of a knitting needle. Make the leaf-shaped wings and attach them behind the shoulders. Roll out a thin piece of dough and attach part of it behind the head for the halo, using the remaining piece to decorate the hem of the dress (Sketch 33c). Shape two rolls for arms and place a simple bouquet between them (see Photo 12). Make a few thin rolls for the hair (or press dough through a garlic press) and make the facial features with a knitting needle.

The angels are made of natural-coloured dough with just a few strokes of paint on the face, bouquet, hem and wings. The yellowish colour is a result of a thick layer of varnish.

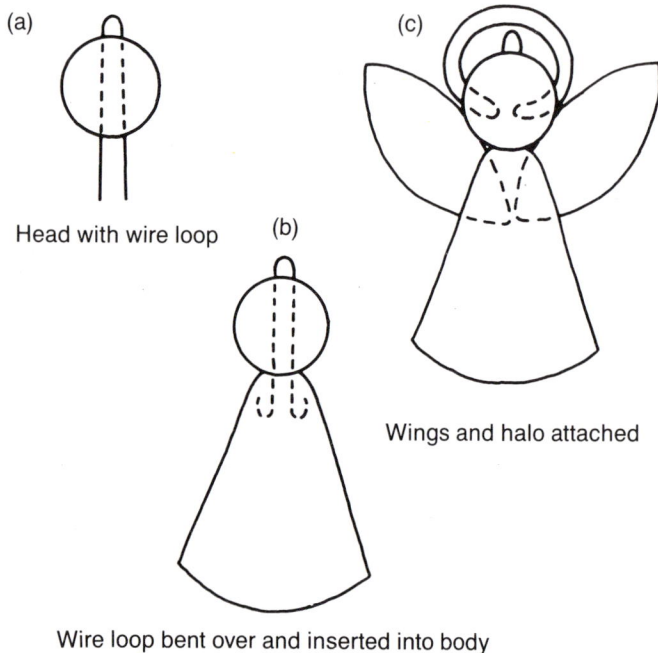

Photo 12

(a) Head with wire loop

(b) Wire loop bent over and inserted into body

(c) Wings and halo attached

Sketch 33: How to assemble the angel

Choir boys

Size: 16,5 cm high

First shape the window opening in which the three choir boys are standing. Roll out two pieces of dough, 3 mm and 6 mm thick respectively, and cut out the outlines of the curved background from each one (Template 10 on p. 32). Now place the pattern over each of the two cut-out pieces again. Cut out the following parts after marking the lines with pin pricks on the dough. On the thicker piece, cut out the entire middle section so that only the curved edge remains. On the thinner piece, cut out only the three peaked window openings. The clover-leaf motifs between the windows are made with the cap of a pen. Now place the border of thicker dough on top of the thinner piece and press it down firmly.

Place the heads and bodies of the figures on the lower part of the thinner piece which has not been cut away. The dough for the figures should be more or less as thick as the frame. Cut the collars, books and hair from thinly rolled-out dough and place the arms in the appropriate places. Shape the eyes and singing mouths with a knitting needle.

Paint the figures after they have been baked, or simply use a few splashes of colour to brighten them, as on Photo 13.

Photo 13

Country girls

Size: About 14 cm high

These charming girls are made from plain dough combined with dough that has been coloured yellow, brown and various shades of green. As with most of the other figures, one begins with the heads, followed by the bodice, skirt, arms, hair and accessories. They are not all that easy to make, however, as the effect depends on the draping of the wide, pleated dresses and ribbons. Handy hints are to make a very stiff dough and not to roll the dough for the dress too thinly – between 2 mm and 3 mm thick.

For each skirt, cut a rectangle from the rolled-out dough, about 15 cm long and as wide as the length of the dress.

Pleat it on one of the long sides and attach to the waist. Make sure that the dough on the sides of the skirt curls around to the back so that the edge is not visible. Do not try to make the pleats in the skirt exactly the same as in the photo; allow the dough to drape naturally – with a bit of assistance. To give the skirt volume, fill up from the back with pieces of dough. The white frill at the bottom of yellow dress is actually a longer white skirt extending beyond the top dress. Give this girl an ordinary bonnet shaped from an oblong semicircle (see p. 8). Give the girl in green a bonnet with a pleated crown and a broad pleated brim. Shape these separately (see Sketch 34 and Template 12 on p. 32). Press dough through a sieve for the hair.

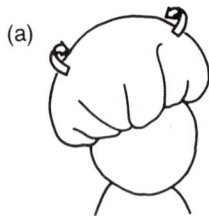

(a) Crown pleated and attached to head

(b) Crown folded back

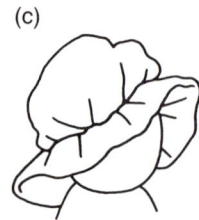

(c) Pleated brim attached

Sketch 34: How to make the green bonnet

Photo 14

Templates

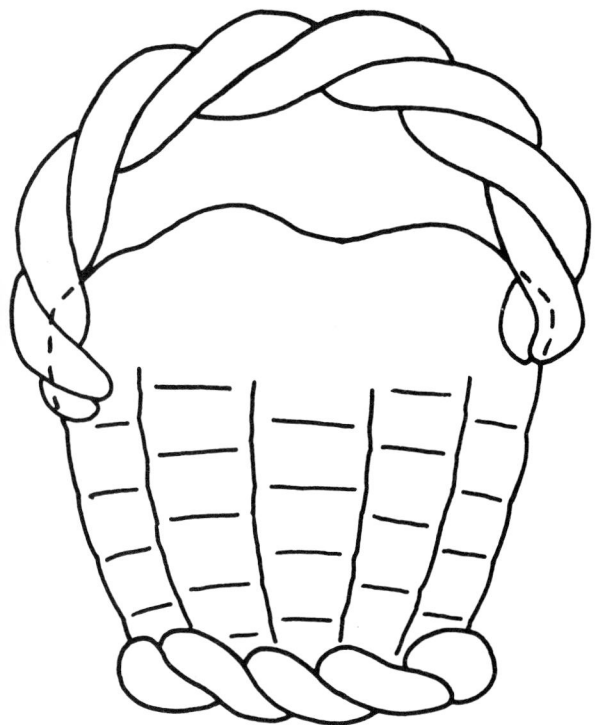

Template 1: 9,5 cm basket (p. 12)

Template 2: Dark brown tree (p. 17)

Template 3: Tree in pastel colours (p. 17)

Template 4: Shapes for heart mobile (p. 19)

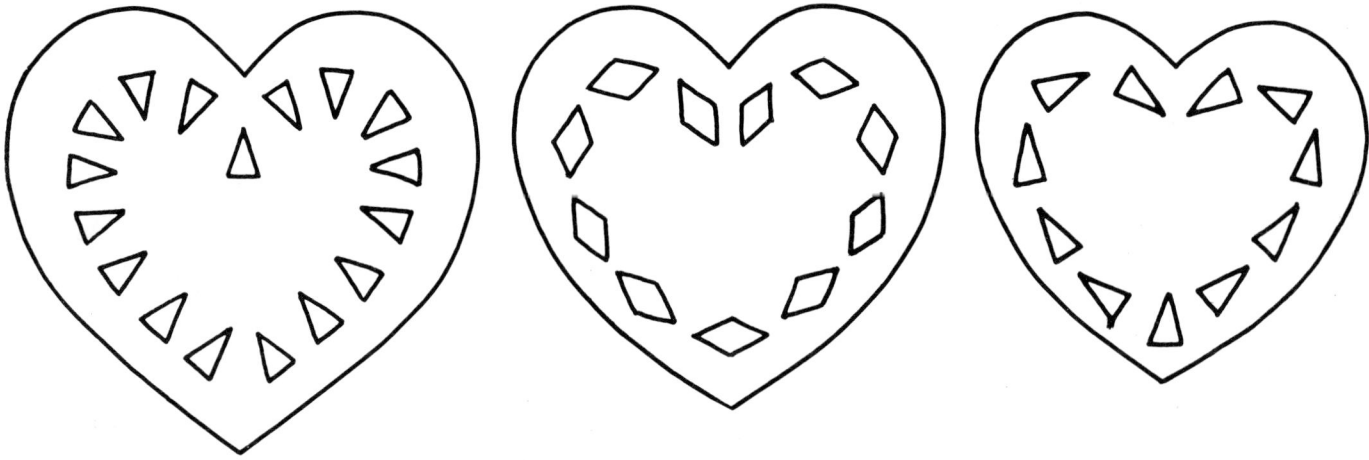

Template 5: Shapes for heart mobile (p. 19)

Template 6: Cottage (p. 17)

Template 7: Shapes for guineafowl mobile (p. 20)

Template 8: Christmas decorations (p. 25)

Border of thick dough

Window opening

Window opening

Window opening

Position of heads

Background made with thin dough

Template 10: Base for choir boys (p. 26)

Template 9: Christmas decorations (p. 25)

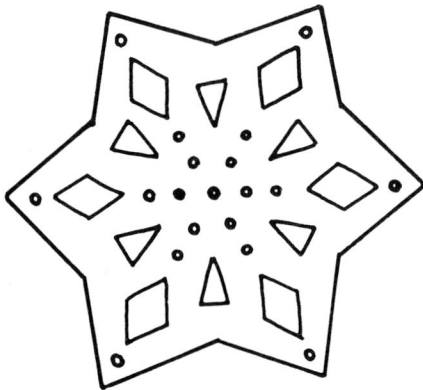

Template 11: Christmas decorations (p. 25)

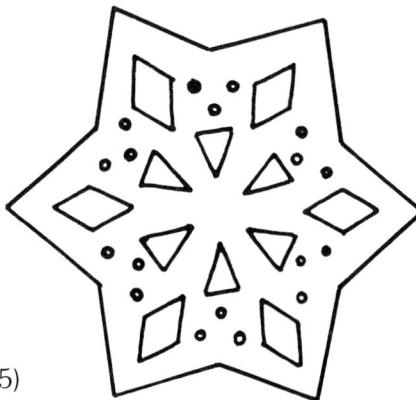

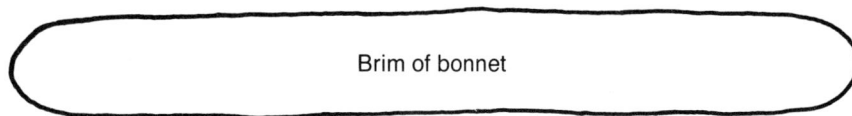

Brim of bonnet

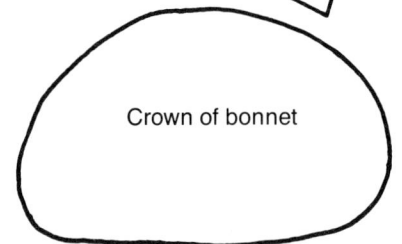

Crown of bonnet

Template 12: Country girl's bonnet (p. 28)

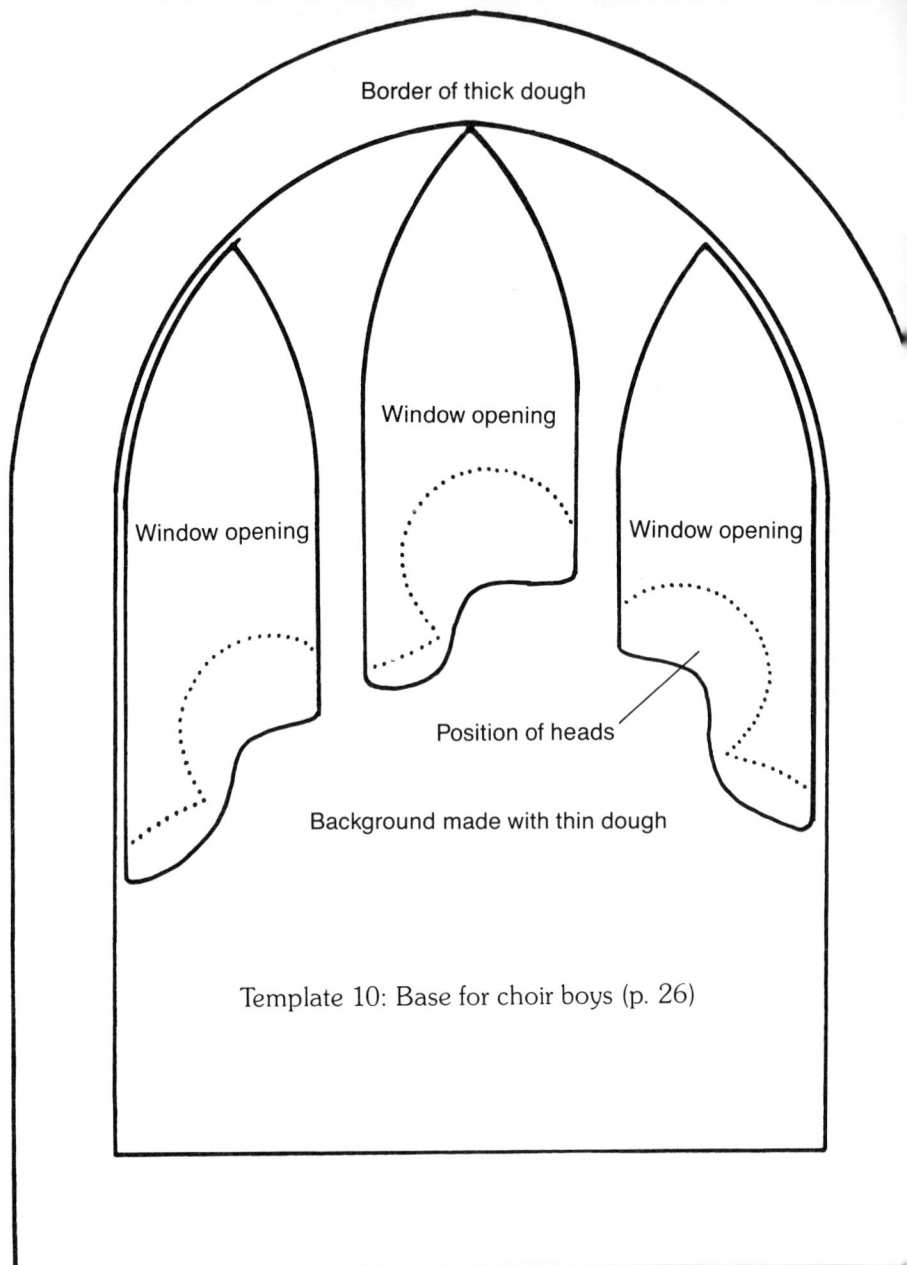